JUST A FEW THINGS I LOVE ABOUT YOU (UNDER THE TREE)

LARKINROAD

ISBN: 978-2-6493-6404-0

you're my favorite gift this season
To:
Love:
A note from me to you:

ONE THING I'M EXCITED ABOUT FOR THE

NEW YEAR

WITH YOU

THREE REASONS I'M
GRATEFUL
FOR YOU
1.
2.
3.

IF THERE WAS A HOLIDAY

MOVIE

ABOUT US,
THE TITLE WOULD BE

One thing
about you
that I'll never
take for granted

YOU MADE THIS
HOLIDAY
SEASON
FUN WHEN YOU
cocoa

ONE SILLY
memory of us
THAT ALWAYS MAKES
me
SMILE

BEST GIFT
YOU'VE GIVEN ME
THAT MONEY CAN'T BUY

ONE
QUALITY
OF YOURS
THAT I ADORE

BEST
COMPLIMENT
YOU'VE EVER GIVEN ME

SOMETHING
YOU DO
THAT MAKES
MY DAYS
BRIGHTER

ONE
GIFT
YOU'VE GIVEN ME
THAT I'LL ALWAYS
REMEMBER

ONE
SMALL
MOMENT
I LOVED SHARING
WITH YOU THIS YEAR

MY
FAVORITE
JOKE
WE SHARE

YOU SHOULD WIN THIS
AWARD

ONE WAY THAT
YOU'VE CHANGED
MY LIFE FOR THE
BETTER

SOMETHING *SMALL*

YOU DO THAT MAKES A BIG DIFFERENCE

YOU MAKE
EVERYTHING
SWEETER
WHEN YOU

IF I COULD GIVE YOU ONE
MAGICAL
GIFT
IT WOULD BE

I'M
PROUD OF
YOU FOR

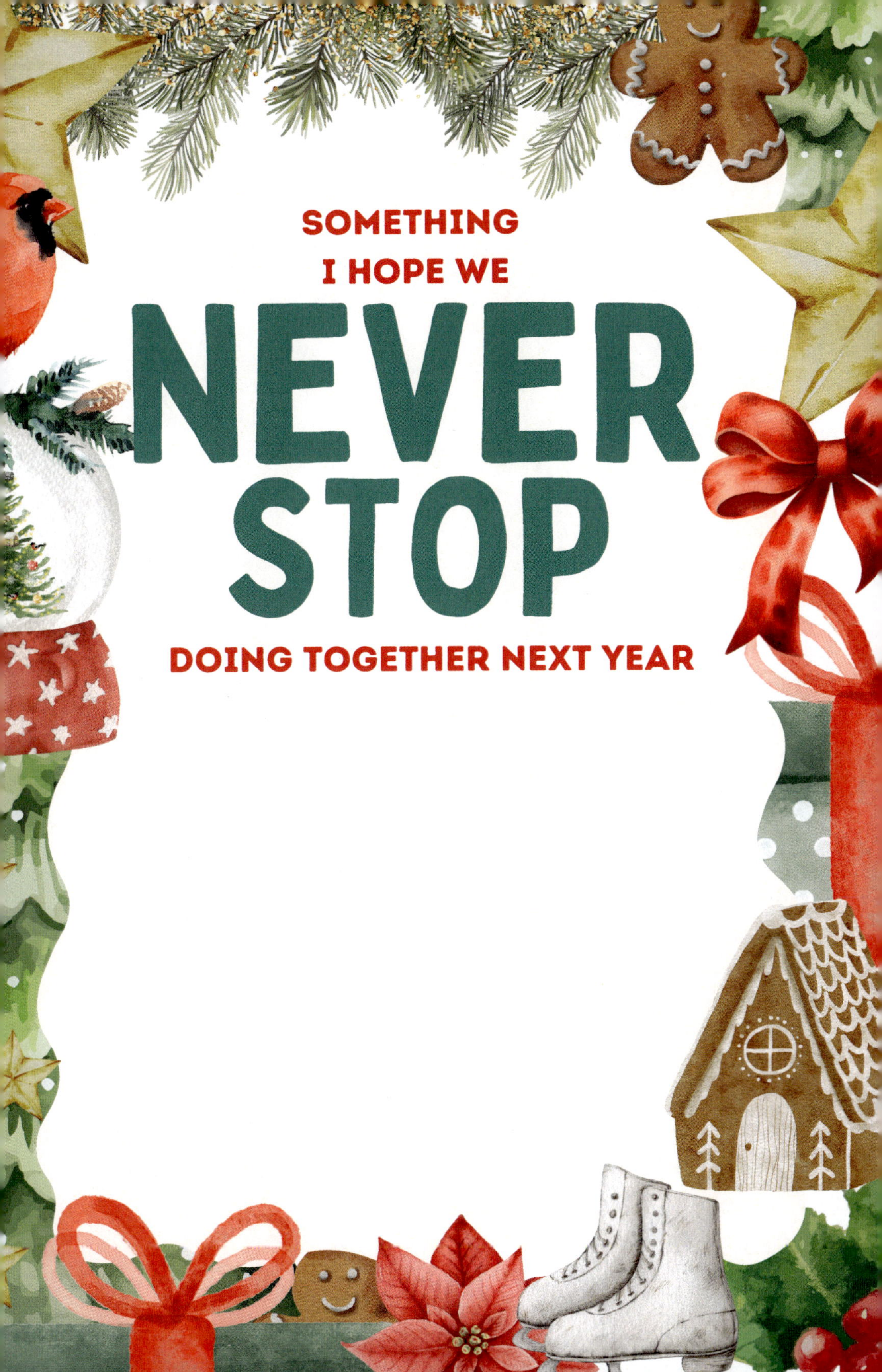

SOMETHING
I HOPE WE
NEVER
STOP
DOING TOGETHER NEXT YEAR

Made in the USA
Coppell, TX
20 December 2025

66676480R00029